Elvis
and the
Talent
Show

Charles Weaver

Fulton Books, Inc.
Meadville, PA

Published by Fulton Books 2021

ISBN 978-1-64952-364-8 (paperback)
ISBN 978-1-64952-365-5 (digital)

Printed in the United States of America

Elvis
and the
Talent
Show

CHARLES WEAVER

It's well known that Elvis Presley had a knack for singing songs.
Blues, jazz, and gospel, he just really couldn't go wrong.
From a young age, people knew that he had something unique.
His early years before he was king, let's take a little peek.

We'll travel back to when he was born in January 1935.
He owned the room (even then) at only five minutes alive.
His doc slapped his bottom, and Elvis didn't think that was cool.
He screamed and wailed and it sounded like "Hey Man, Don't Be Cruel."

1

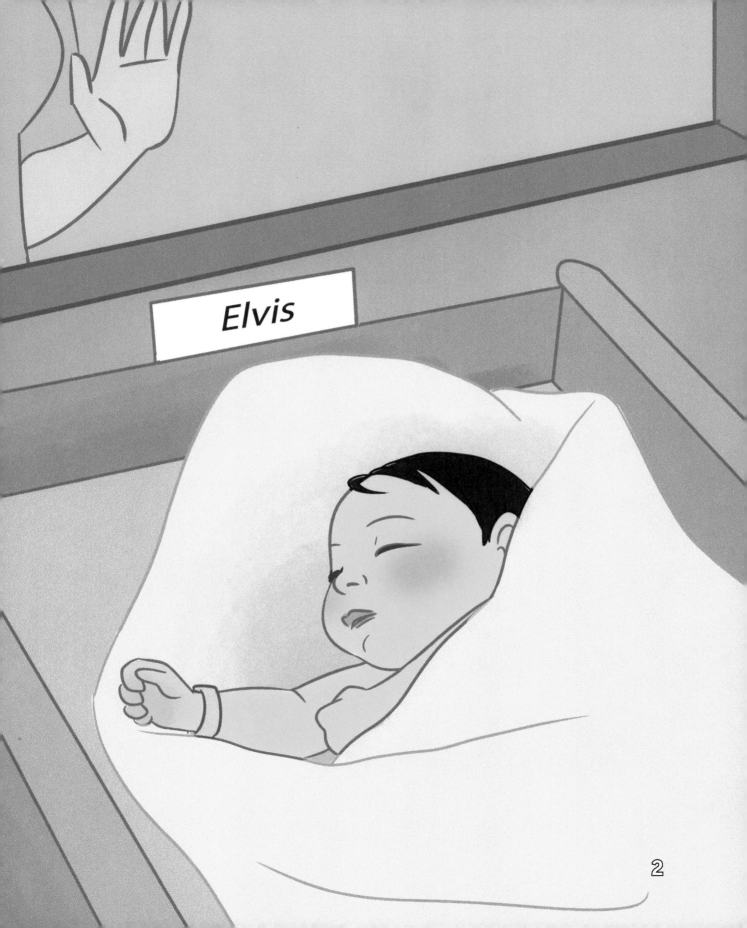

Elvis

2

State Fair this Saturd
Talent Show

$14 + 12 = 26$

$16 - 7 = 9$

$3 \cdot 9 = 27$

$3 - 4 + 5 = 4$

$2 \cdot 9 = 18$

$3 \cdot 12 = 56$

$9 \cdot 2 = 18$

$7 - 3 = 4$

$2 + 3 = 5$

When Elvis got a little older, people began to see
That he could sing, and he could dance much better than you or me.
It was in school in the fourth grade that his teacher heard his voice.
She suggested he enter a talent show, and he made a simple choice.

The talent show was to take place at the Mississippi fair.
Elvis played some games and won his mama a big pink "Teddy Bear."
She hugged it close when he gave it to her with a big gleam in his eye.
Those are the feelings, his mama knew, that no money could buy.

After the games, they went into a tent where souvenirs were sold.
An old gypsy woman in the corner with a sign that said "Fortunes Told."
Little Elvis wanted to talk to her, but his mama grabbed his arm.
She handed him a penny and said, "There's your Good Luck Charm."

6

The talent show would be at four, and they needed to eat some lunch.
At a state fair, there is always plenty of tasty food to munch.
Elvis had a corn dog and fries; his mom had the same.
He was only three hours away from his first brush with fame.

After lunch, Elvis decided to ride a couple of rides.
Probably not the best decision since his corn dog was still inside.
He got in line for a ride that would spin him in a teacup.
When he was done, you could say that he was "All Shook Up."

He and his mama took a rest, and he was still a bit queasy.
After a while, he felt better but was still a little uneasy.
The talent show was an hour away, and he knew he had to be ready.
Elvis was a little nervous, but he was focused, and he was steady.

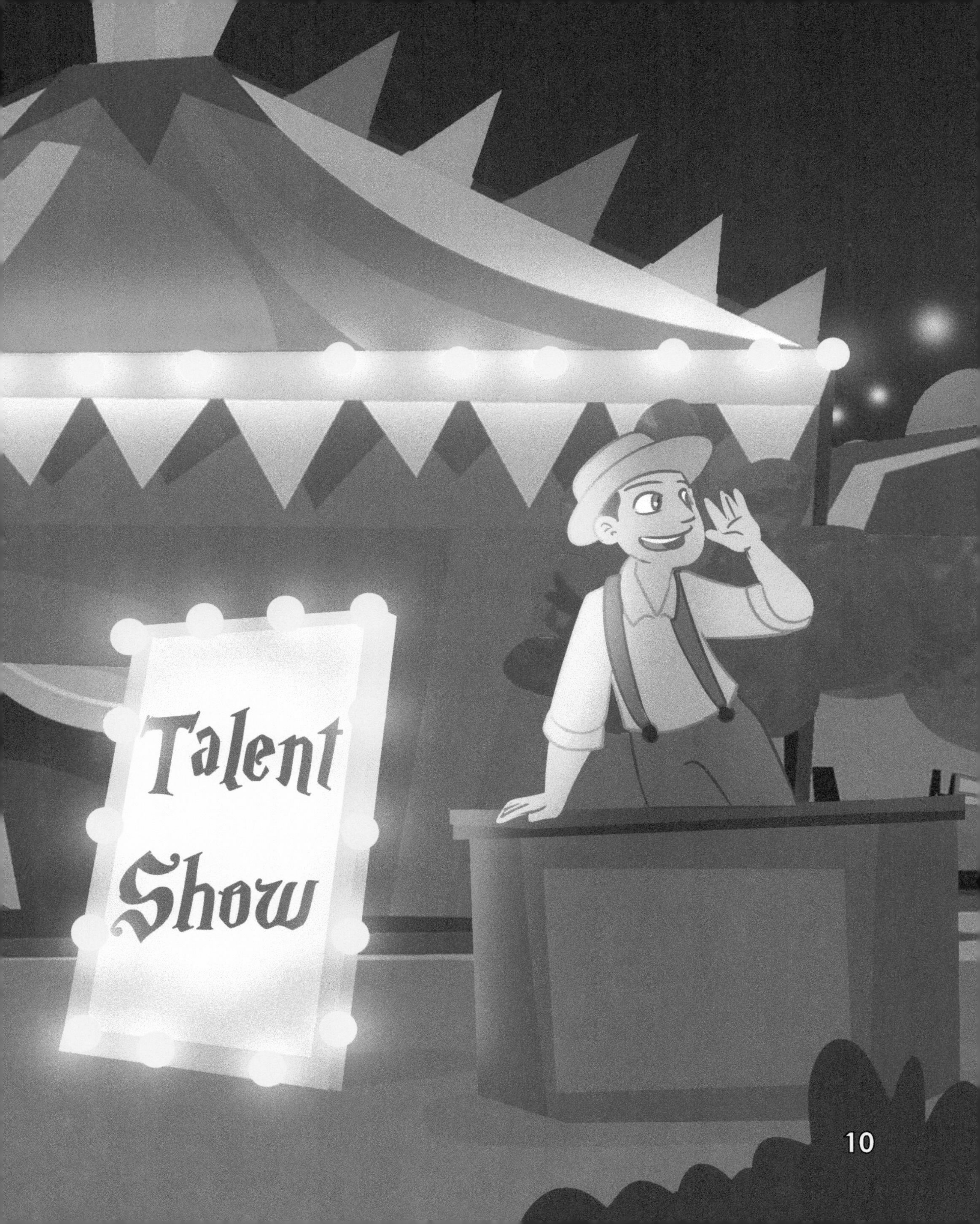
Talent Show

Walking to the stage where the show would be taking place.
Elvis breathed in the cotton-candy air and felt the setting sun on his face.
Arriving at the tent to sign up, they had to stand in line.
There were twenty acts that were to perform, and he was number 9.

While sitting backstage with his mom, Elvis was able to see
The acts that went before him and many filled him with glee,
Like one with dancing poodles and another with a jumping frog.
There was even one with a piano-playing brown-and-white "Hound Dog."

11

The time finally arrived when Elvis was the next one to go on.
He kissed his mama, grabbed his hat, and got ready to sing his song.
He was still a bit jittery and shaky (he was only nine after all).
But when he took the stage to sing his song, he felt ten feet tall.

The microphone was too high for him, and he had to stand on a chair.
To sing his song called "Old Shep," and he was quite aware
That the crowd was loud; they loved his song, and he thought that he might win.
It ended so quickly that he asked the crowd if he could sing it again.

When he was done, the audience cheered, and he felt very proud.
He went backstage and tried to find his mom there in the crowd.
He looked around and found her with tears streaming down her face.
There were no words needed, just a loving mother and son embrace.

13

Now keep in mind that Elvis was the ninth act to perform,
Which meant about a dozen more acts, and the night was getting warm.
But Elvis and his mama sat through every song and dance.
And Elvis wanted to win, and he thought he had a good chance.

The show was finally over, and the judges tallied their votes.
Dogs and people were sitting there with the highest hopes.
Little Elvis sat with his mama and waited what seemed forever.
Someone in the audience shouted, "Come on, It's Now or Never!"

Twenty acts, and Elvis was told that he was in the top 5.

He hugged his momma, and the crowd cheered; it was great to be alive.

When the winner was announced, he didn't come out on top.

Little Elvis, who'd take fifth was disappointed, but he wouldn't stop.

Even though in the end, the dancing poodles were the winner,
Elvis would recall, as he and his mom ate a late dinner,
That winning isn't everything, and he was not about to cry.
The only true losers are the ones that won't even try.

Lorem ipsum

Lorem ipsum dolor sit
amet, id tation feugait
commune vel, ne vix
epicurei constituto.

20

A few months later, Elvis would receive his very first guitar.
Some boys would have preferred a bicycle or even a model car.
But that night at the fair showed Elvis what his true calling would be.
To bring the gift of rock and roll to folks like you and me.

22

23

This is a story of fiction with real elements of truth. Elvis Presley did enter a talent show at the Mississippi/Alabama State Fair at the age of nine or ten. He did place fifth, wore a cowboy hat, and really had to stand on a chair to reach the microphone. The name of the song he sang was "Old Shep." He also really received his first guitar a few months later, but by most accounts would have preferred a bicycle or an air rifle.

About the Author

Elvis and the Talent Show is Charles Weaver's first published book. Charles lives in Flushing, Michigan, with his wife, Katrina, and his two daughters, Jillian and Charlotte. He has been an elementary school teacher for the last twenty-two years, teaching third through sixth grades during that time. His love of Elvis Presley can be attributed to his big brother Frank. He grew up in Flint and graduated from the University of Michigan. Go, Blue! When he isn't writing children's books, he enjoys traveling around the country with his family and playing with the family's new dog, Freddie Mercury.

CPSIA information can be obtained
at www.ICGtesting.com
Printed in the USA
JSHW042052281220
10619JS00002B/70